SOCIAL SCIENCE
PRIMARY 1

BY ME

ACTIVITY BOOK

CB123071

UNIT 1 My school

1 Say and trace.

classroom

playground

library

dining hall

gym

toilets

2 Write.

caretaker   cook   ~~teacher~~

The teacher teaches the pupils in the classroom.

The ________ prepares and serves food in the dining hall.

The ________ keeps the school tidy.

3 Which materials do you need? Trace and match.

rubber

pencil sharpener

crayons

4 Trace. Circle the correct objects.

Art

Music

P.E.

Science

5 Write.

write draw play paint eat ~~run~~

run

6 Write. Draw a picture of your favourite school subject.

My name is ______________.

My favourite school subject is ______________.

I like to ______________ in the playground.

My favourite school subject

7 Who is being a good friend? Put a tick (✓) or a cross (✗).

8 Trace and match.

Put your hand up.

Keep your classroom tidy.

Line up.

Let's investigate at home!

Make a *Ready for school* mini book

1

Cut out and fold your mini book.

2

Draw pictures.

3

Write sentences.

4

Decorate the cover.

1 Write *yes* or *no*.

Do you brush your teeth? ____________

Do you check your school bag? ____________

Skills check

1 Look and read. Put a tick (✓) or a cross (✗). Look at the two examples.

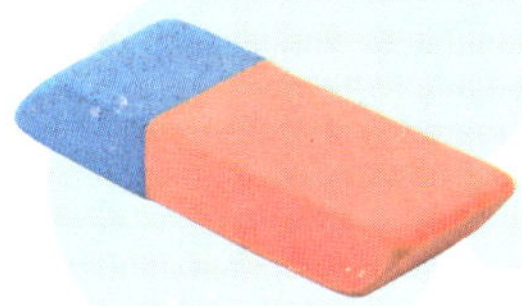

This is a rubber. ✓

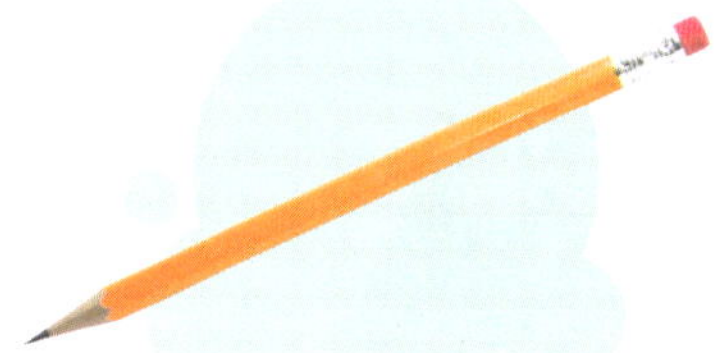

This is a book. ✗

1 This is a computer. ☐

2 These are paints. ☐

3 This is a poster. ☐

4 This is a ball. ☐

5 This is a ruler. ☐

UNIT 2 My home

1 Write.

flat window roof wall ~~house~~ door

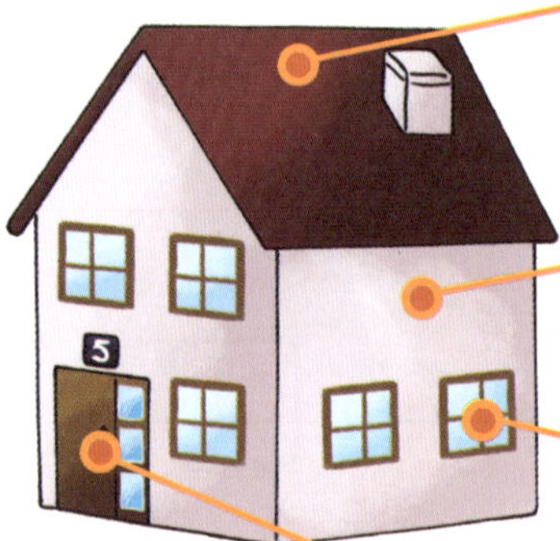

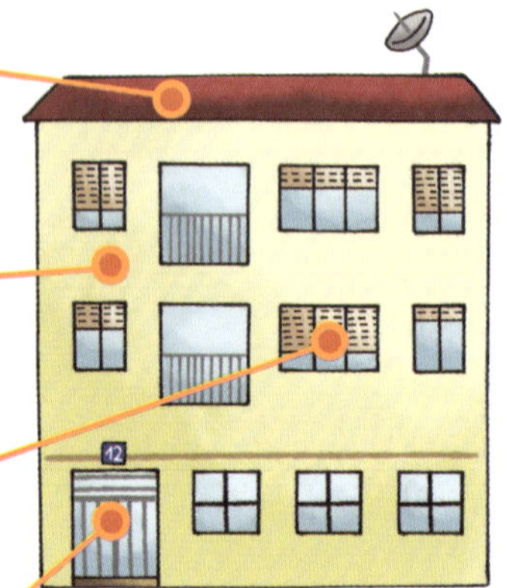

house

2 Write.

1

2 B

A

3 T

H

4 R

O

O

M

3 Colour.

kitchen living room bedroom bathroom

  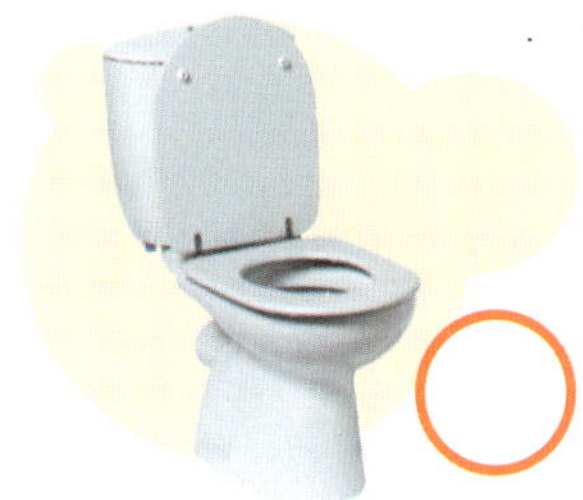 

 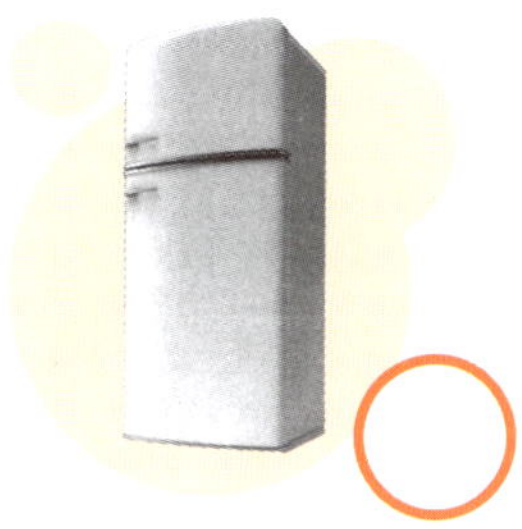  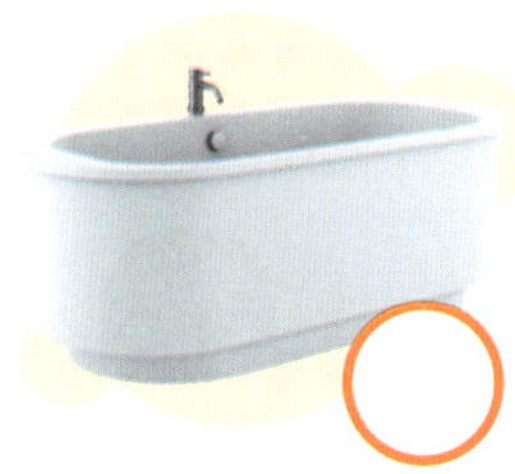

4 Trace and match.

The oven and the fridge are in the kitchen.

The bed and the wardrobe are in the bedroom.

The sofa and the television are in the living room.

5 Write.

cousins father grandmother sister uncle brother

grandfather

mother

aunt

6 Circle the family members.

sisterkitchencousinsauntbedgrandfatherwardrobeunclemother

7 Read and circle the correct word.

I wash/make the bed.

I lay/make the table.

I help in the kitchen/bedroom.

I water/wash the dishes.

I water/wash the plants.

I make the bed/tidy up.

8 Trace. Say who is doing each job.

wash the dishes

make the bed

tidy up

Let's investigate at home!

Make a *Help at home* chart

1

Design and colour your chart.

2

Put it in the kitchen.

3

Do the jobs on your chart every day.

4

Put a sticker on your chart when you help at home.

1 Write.

Do you help at home every day? ____________

What is your favourite job? ____________

Skills check

1 Look at the pictures. Look at the letters. Write the words.

f r i d g e

i e f g r d

1 

....

h u e s o

2 

....

b r e r w d a o

3 

....

n e c l u

4 

....

i w w d n o

5 

....

s o c i n u s

UNIT 3

Where I live

1 Trace and match.

road sign

pavement

traffic lights

2 Colour. Find the words.

road

green man

red man

car

q	g	a	d	z	b
s	r	c	k	l	h
h	e	r	j	i	w
r	e	d	m	a	n
o	n	w	a	p	c
a	m	e	m	a	t
d	a	a	c	a	r
e	n	s	d	o	f

3 Look and write.

The supermarket is at 9 Park Road.

I live at ______________________.

My best friend lives at ______________________.

The chemist's is at ______________________.

The church is at ______________________.

4 Where do we find these things? Write *yes* or *no*.

	in a city	in a village	city and village
	no		

5 Circle and write.

museum | swimming pool

I swim in the swimming pool.

park | post office

I play in the ______.

school | supermarket

I study at ______.

library | bank

I read in the ______.

6 Write and match.

pedestrian crossing ~~bin~~ green man

Throw your rubbish in the bin.

Use a ______ to cross the road.

Wait for the ______ before you cross the road.

7 Do they travel on land, on water or in the air? Write.

boat

lorry

helicopter

plane

bicycle

cargo ship

lorry		

Let's investigate at home!

Invent a new type of transport

1

Draw the body of your new type of transport.

2

Add wheels and windows.

3

Add more details.

4

Colour and cut out your picture.

1 Write.

My new type of transport has ________ wheels.
It has ________ windows.

Skills check

1 Look at the pictures. Look at the letters. Write the words.

s c h o o l

school
scohol

1 

…… …… …… …… …… ……

cuhrch
church

2 

…… …… …… …… …… …… …… ……

pevament
pavement

3 

…… …… …… …… …… …… ……

library
libarry

4 

…… …… …… …… …… …… ……

village
villaeg

5 

…… …… …… …… …… …… ……
…… …… …… …… …… ……

traffic lights
triffac litghs

UNIT 4 The world around us

1 Look and write.

l a k e

e a k l

l i n p a

c a e h b

f c i f l

s f r e o t

e s a

2 Write the features above in the correct group.

inland landscape	coastal landscape
lake	

3 Trace and colour.

natural man-made

house

tree

fence

flowers

windmill

bridge

4 Circle the things that need air.

snail

duck

person

van

poster

road sign

cow

oven

5 Write.

cloud

rain

snow

lake

ice

sea

solid	liquid	gas
	rain	

6 Write.

drink ~~clean~~ hands wash

We use water to clean the floor.

We use water to wash our ______.

We use water to ______ food.

We ______ water when we are thirsty.

7 Write.

1

2

3

4

5

1 S T O R M Y

2

3

4

5

8 What is the hidden word? ....

9 Read and draw.

1. It is cloudy in Barcelona.
2. It is snowy in Bilbao.
3. It is rainy in Madrid.
4. It is sunny in Sevilla.
5. It is windy in Valencia.

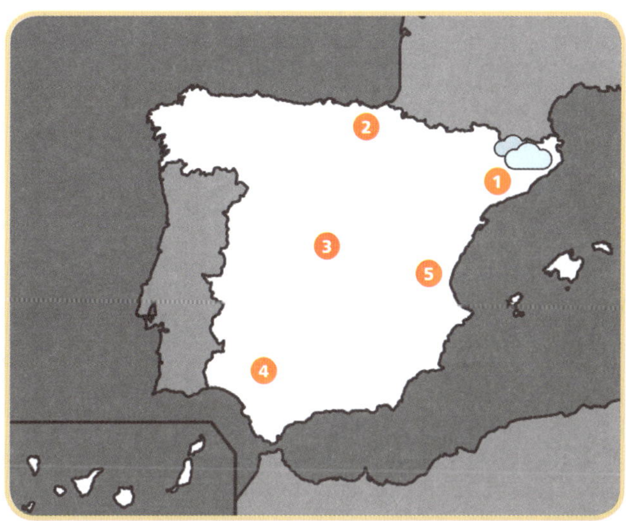

Let's investigate at home!

Make a weather wheel

1

Cut out two circles.

2

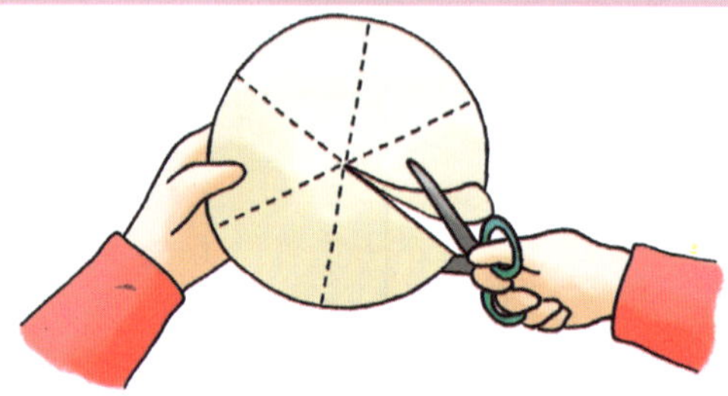

Divide one circle into six parts.
Cut out one part.

3

Draw and colour six different
types of weather.

4

Fasten the two circles together.
Decorate the top circle.

1 Write.

What is the weather like today? ______

What is your favourite type of weather? ______

Skills check

1 Look and read. Write *yes* or *no*.

Example: There is a man in the bedroom. no

1. Trees are man-made features of a landscape.
2. A dog needs air to live.
3. We use water to wash our hands.
4. The weather is snowy in the picture.

UNIT 5 The Sun and the Moon

① Say and trace. Match.

clouds

Earth

Sun

stars

Moon

planet

② What can we see in the sky? Look and write.

r t a s s — s t a r s

p t l a e n — ....

o M o n — ....

a r E t h — ....

d o l c u s — ....

3 Read and trace. Circle the correct answers.

1 Which objects are round?

 Moon

 book

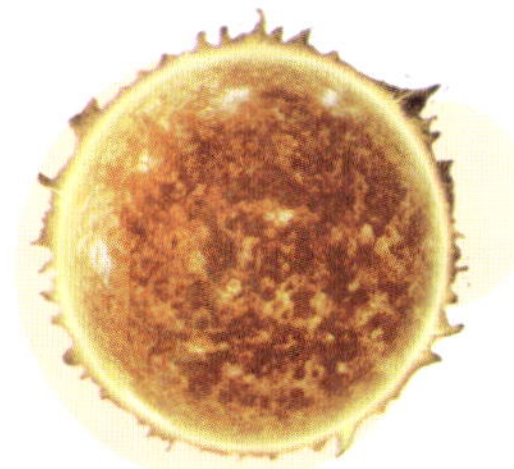 Sun

 van

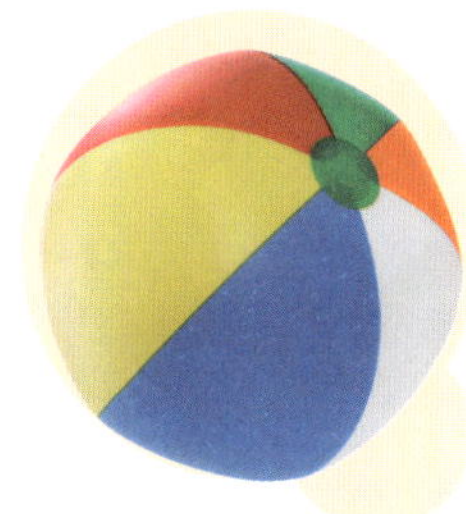 ball

2 Which objects give us light?

 light bulb

 rubber

 ice cream

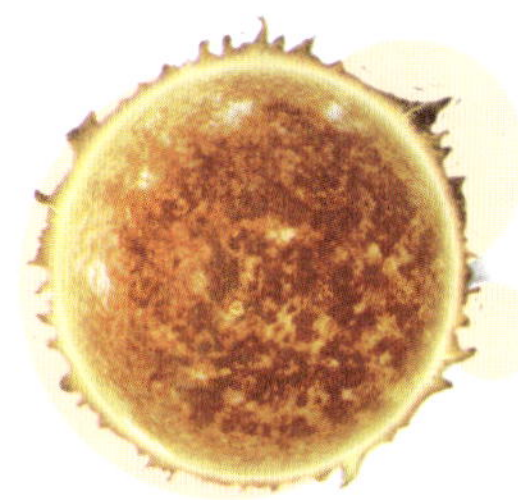 Sun

 fire

3 Which objects give us heat?

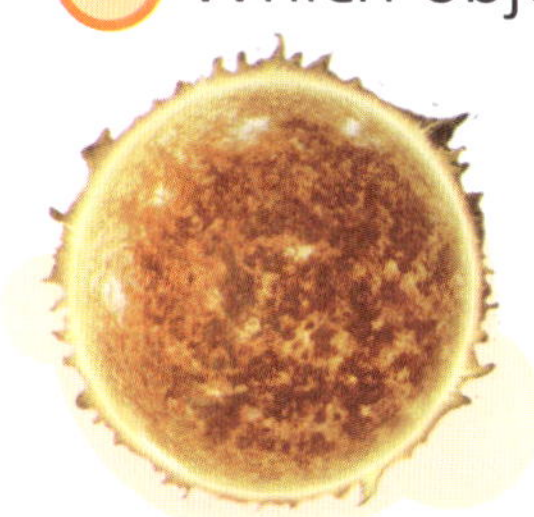 Sun

 fire

 bench

 Moon

 radiator

4 Look at activity 3. Write the correct word.

The .... is round. It gives us light and heat.

5 Trace. Use the code and colour.

The Earth moves around the Sun.

The Moon moves around the Earth.

6 Trace and write.

winter ~~summer~~ spring autumn

	summer		
March	June	September	December
April	July	October	January
May	August	November	February

7 Tick.

8 Look at activity 7. Write.

1. In Canada, Kevin is waking up.
2. In Spain, Paula is ________.
3. In China, Mei is ________.

~~waking up~~
sleeping
studying

9 Read and put a tick or a cross.

1. The Earth moves around the Moon. ✗
2. The Sun is a star. ☐
3. There are ten months in a year. ☐
4. The Moon changes shape. ☐
5. The Moon is made of rocks. ☐

Let's investigate at home!

Record the moon for a month

1

Make a calendar.

2

Observe the moon every night.

3

Draw a picture of the moon on your calendar.

4

Colour and decorate your calendar.

1 **Write *yes* or *no*.**

Does the moon always look round? ____________

Does the moon give us heat? ____________

Skills check

1 **Read. Choose a word or phrase from the box and write.**

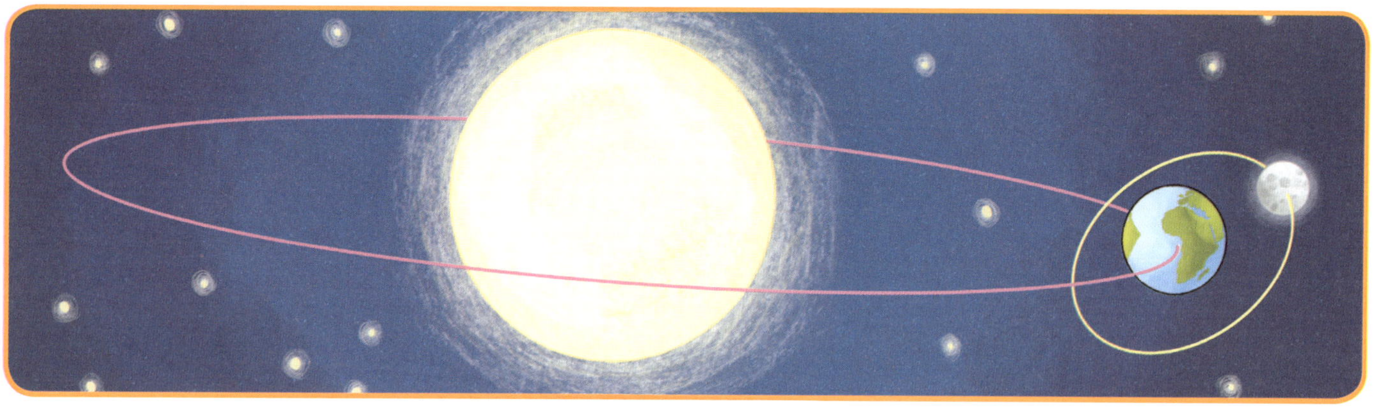

We live on the Earth. During the day we can see the (1) ______. In the morning I wake up and I (2) ______ ______. At night we can see the (3) ______. We can also see lots of (4) ______. At night I (5) ______.

stars

go to bed

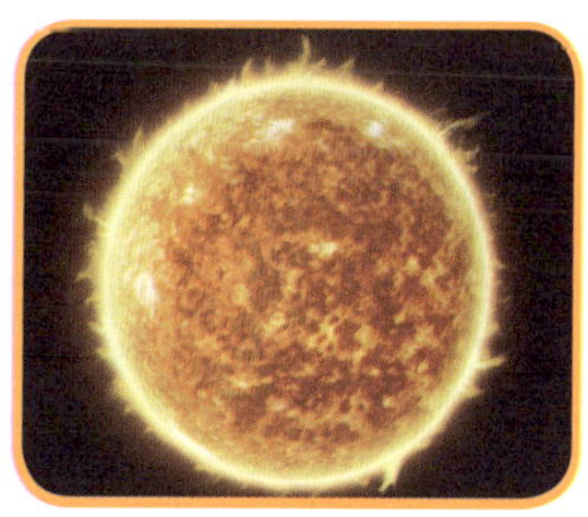
Sun

crater

summer

Moon

go to school

Earth

UNIT 6 Time

1 Put a tick or a cross.

1 

2 

3 

This is a baby. ✓

This is a child. ☐

This is an adult. ☐

2 Write the family members.

brother mother ~~me~~ grandmother great-grandfather
father great-grandmother grandfather sister

1. me
2. ______
3. ______
4. ______
5. ______
6. ______
7. ______
8. ______
9. ______

3 Put the pictures in order. Write numbers.

1

 1

2

4 Write and draw.

computer fridge shoes ~~car~~

	past	present	future
car			

UNIT 6

5 Match.

morning

afternoon

evening

6 Write.

Saturday Tuesday Friday ~~Monday~~ Sunday Thursday Wednesday

Monday				

weekdays

weekend

7 Trace and match.

spring — summer — autumn — winter

8 Colour.

spring summer autumn winter

December June September February May

March July October November

January April August

9 Write the correct number.

1. There are f o u r seasons in a year.
2. There are ... ... months in a season.
3. There are ... ... months in a year.
4. There are ... ... days in a week.

12 7

3 ~~4~~

Let's investigate at home!

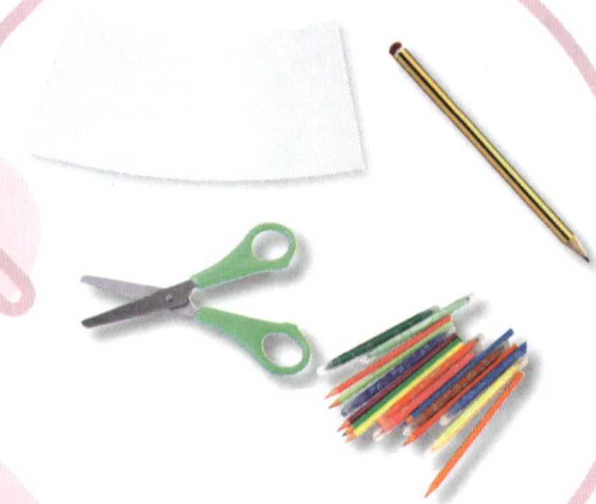

Make a four seasons album

1. 

Cut out your album.

2. 

Fold on the lines.

3. 

Draw pictures of things from the different seasons.

4. 

Decorate the cover of your album.

1 Write.

What is your favourite season? ____________________

What is the weather like in your favourite season? ____________________

Skills check

1 Look and read. Write *yes* or *no*.

Example: The boy is doing his homework. ___yes___

1. The woman is sleeping. ______
2. The man is watching television. ______
3. There are three photos on the wall. ______
4. It is Wednesday in the picture. ______
5. It is summer in the picture. ______

Glossary

English	Your language

UNIT 1: My school

classroom	
dining hall	
playground	
gym	
library	
toilets	
Science	
Art	
Music	
P.E.	

UNIT 2: My home

house	
flat	
bathroom	
bedroom	
kitchen	
living room	
furniture	

English	Your language

UNIT 3: Where I live

city	
village	
pavement	
pedestrian crossing	
green man	
traffic lights	
road sign	

UNIT 4: The world around us

forest	
plain	
beach	
cliff	
bridge	
windmill	
cloudy	
foggy	
snowy	
stormy	

Glossary

English	Your language
UNIT 5: The Sun and the Moon	
Sun	
Earth	
Moon	
crater	
planet	
star	
astronaut	
UNIT 6: Time	
grandparents	
great-grandparents	
yesterday	
tomorrow	
weekend	
spring	
summer	
autumn	
winter	